SIMPLY **SCIENCE**

The Simple Science of

DIRT

by Emily James

CAPSTONE PRESS
a capstone imprint

A+ Books are published by Capstone Press,
1710 Roe Crest Drive, North Mankato, Minnesota 56003
www.mycapstone.com

Library of Congress Cataloging-in-Publication Data
Cataloging-in-publication information is on file with the Library of Congress.
ISBN 978-1-5157-7085-5 (library binding)
ISBN 978-1-5157-7092-3 (paperback)
ISBN 978-1-5157-7100-5 (eBook PDF)

Editorial Credits
Jaclyn Jaycox, editor; Jenny Bergstrom, designer; Jo Miller, media researcher; Tori Abraham, production specialist

Photo Credits
Shutterstock: Alexander Bark, 8-9, Antonov Roman, 16-17, dnaveh, 26-27, Dragon Images, 24-25, Drakuliren, 22-23, Elvan, 21, Fabio Lamanna, 10-11, fotoslaz, 28-29, GalapagosPhoto, cover, George Dolgikh, 14-15, LexRiver, 7, marcovarro, 18-19, MR.RAWIN TANPIN, 6, Nick Biemans, 20, Riccardo Arata, 12-13, showcake, 13 (inset), spiphotoone, 23 (inset), Sujalmages, 29 (inset), Suzanne Tucker, 4-5

Design Elements
Shutterstock: diogoppr, xpixel

Note to Parents, Teachers, and Librarians

This Simply Science book uses full color photographs and a nonfiction format to introduce the concept of dirt. *The Simple Science of Dirt* is designed to be read aloud to a pre-reader or to be read independently by an early reader. Photographs help listeners and early readers understand the text and concepts discussed. The book encourages further learning by including the following sections: Table of Contents, Glossary, Read More, Internet Sites, and Index. Early readers may need assistance using these features.

Table of
CONTENTS

What Is Dirt?

Look! Under your feet. What do you see?
Dirt! Dirt can be squishy, muddy,
or sandy.

You can dig, play, and plant flowers in it.
Dirt covers almost all the land on Earth.
But what is dirt?

Dirt is also called soil. Soil is a mix of different parts of nature. Rocks form one part. Sand, silt, and clay are pieces of rock that make up soil.

Pieces of leaves and twigs also make up soil. So do tiny parts of animals that lived long ago.

Types of Dirt

Soil found near the ocean is usually made of sand. Sand is mostly broken-down rocks and shells. It feels rough and gritty.

Sand has large grains. They do not stick
together well. Water drains quickly through
sandy soil. This soil does not have many
nutrients. They are carried away by water.

silt

Silt is like sand. But silt's grains are smaller.
It is a dark color. It feels soft and smooth.
Silt is a good soil for growing plants. It holds
a lot of food and water for plants.

Clay has even smaller grains than silt. It can be many colors. It feels soft and sticky. Clay does not drain well. Minerals stick to it. Minerals make clay a good soil for growing crops.

Humus is the dark, gooey part of soil.
It is made from rotting plants,
leaves, wood, and animal matter.

Sticky humus helps hold the rocky parts
of dirt together. Humus contains food that
plants need to grow.

Layers of Dirt

Humus, water, and air are usually found in the upper layer of dirt. This layer is called topsoil.

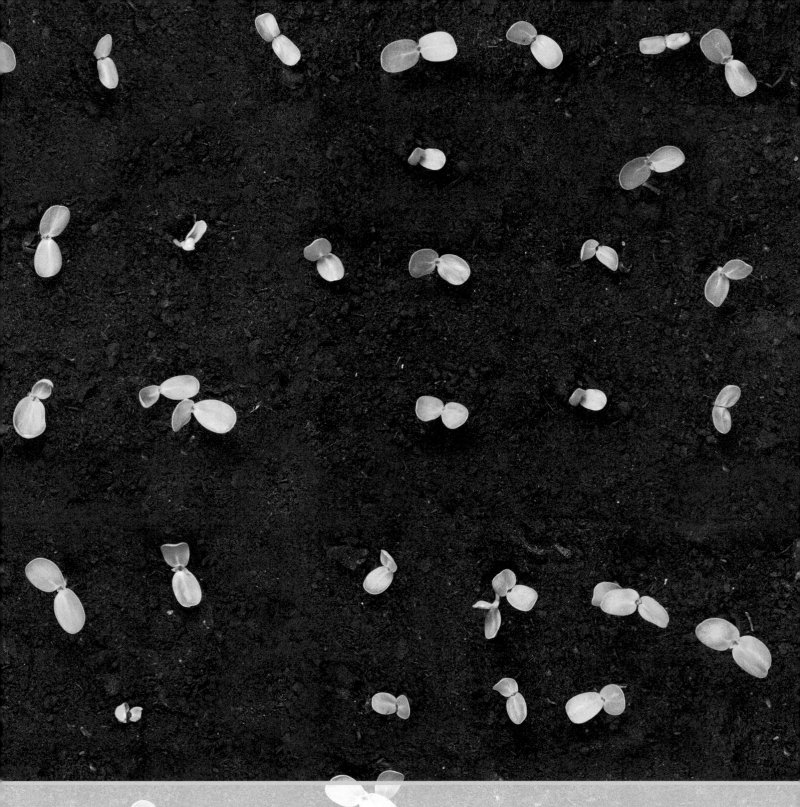

Topsoil is very dark and filled with nutrients. It is the best soil for planting. Topsoil can take hundreds of years to form.

topsoil

subsoil

solid rock layer

Under topsoil is subsoil. Minerals gather
in this layer. The roots of plants reach into
subsoil for food and water.

Deep below subsoil is solid rock.
No plants or animals live in this layer.
Soil forms from this rock.

Who Lives in Dirt?

Millions of creatures live in dirt.
Beetles, millipedes, and worms wriggle
and crawl through it. Many decomposers
are so small that you can't see them.

Decomposers make humus. They eat dead
plants and leave droppings in the soil.
The droppings are like vitamins for plants.

Animals can make soil better for plants.
Snails, snakes, and rabbits burrow into soil
and loosen it.

They make holes that let air and water reach
the roots of thirsty plants.

What Do We Use Dirt For?

People use dirt for many things.

Farmers use it to grow crops.

Engineers use it to build roads and dams.

Clay soil is used to build houses.
Sand is used to make cement.

How Can We Take Care of Dirt?

Plant trees! Roots hold soil together.
Without trees, soil can be washed or blown
away. Leaves help protect soil from too much rain.

Don't litter! Trash can harm soil, plants, and animals. Keeping soil healthy is good for all living things.

Dirt keeps us alive. Without dirt, plants
cannot grow. Without plants, animals
cannot eat. Without plants and animals,
people would have no food.

Dig into dirt. Pile it up and stomp it down.
Plant flowers in it. Let it squish between
your fingers and toes. See how amazing
the world beneath you is!

Dig In!

Soil is all around us. It is in gardens and parks. It is beneath the sidewalks and houses. Soil is not exactly the same everywhere. What is the soil made of where you live?

What You Need:

shovel
white paper plate

What You Do:

- Have an adult help you dig up one shovelful of soil. Make sure you dig down deep to get more than just the topsoil.
- Put the soil on the paper plate and spread it out.
- Look for leaves, sticks, bugs, worms, and rocks. Make a list of all the things you find.

- Pour some water on the area where you dug up the soil. Does the ground hold a puddle for a long time? Or does the water sink right away? What does that tell you about your soil?

GLOSSARY

cement—a gray powder made from crushed limestone and clay

creature—a living being

decomposer—a living thing, such as fungi or bacteria, that feeds on dead plants and animals and turns them into soil

engineer—a person who uses science and math to plan, design, or build

grain—a very small piece of something

humus—the wet, dark part of soil that is made of rotted plants and animals; humus has food that plants need

mineral—a material found in nature that is not an animal or a plant

nutrient—something that is needed by people, animals, and plants to stay healthy and strong

silt—the fine particles of soil that are carried along by flowing water and eventually settle to the bottom of a river or lake

READ MORE

Hagler, Gina. *Step-by-Step Experiments with Soils.* Mankato, Minn.: The Child's World, 2012.

MacAulay, Kelley. *Why Do We Need Soil?* Natural Resources Close-Up. New York: Crabtree Publishing Company, 2014.

Rake, Jody S. *Soil, Silt, and Sand: Layers of the Underground.* Underground Safari. North Mankato, Minn.: Capstone Press, 2016.

INTERNET SITES

FactHound offers a safe, fun way to find Internet sites related to this book.

All of the sites on FactHound have been researched by our staff.

Here's all you do:

Visit *www.facthound.com*

Type in this code: 9781515770855

Super-cool stuff! Check out projects, games and lots more at
www.capstonekids.com

CRITICAL THINKING QUESTIONS

1. Soil found near the ocean is usually sand. What is sand made of?
2. There are three layers of dirt described. What are they?
3. Planting trees and not littering are two very important ways to take care of dirt. What other things do you think you could do?

INDEX